# Style

## *The Ultimate Capsule Wardrobe Fashion Guide to Improve a Lady's Beauty, Elegance, and Charm*

*"Buy less, choose well and make it last."*
*- Vivienne Westwood.*

by

Shea Hendricks

# Copyright & Disclaimer:

# Table of Contents

# Synopsis:

For women out there who are quite frankly fed up with feeling like they have nothing to wear, those who are wasting more time than they would like on a daily basis trying to find an outfit that looks half decent, or those who need a style boost or fresh inspiration for their image, read on...

In this book you will find successfully tried and tested methods to help you discover your unique style on a deeper level, interesting yet beneficial information you never knew before, and step by step plans to guide you from your frustratingly over-flowing wardrobe to fashion freedom.

This book starts from the very basics and leads up to the ins and outs of how to dress affordably well and make a positive impact wherever you go.

It includes solid advice on how to shop and buy, how to dress to flatter your body shape, accessorize for maximum effect and choose the right colors.

It teaches women how to create an ideal clothing plan they wished they knew before, how to continue discovering variety on an independent level once finishing the book, and how to dress well for every occasion from work to play.

If you are looking for a short yet effective book jam packed with useful information on how to create a capsule wardrobe to suit your individual personality and needs, you have found the right place.

This book contains everything women need to know in order to embrace their inner style; valuable long lasting lessons will be learned along the way.

By the end of this investment of a book, readers should have a different perspective, not only on how they dress and perceive themselves, but on life in general...

# Chapter 1    How a Capsule Wardrobe could benefit you:

- Many women today complain about never having any decent outfits to wear, or rarely feel good in what they are wearing. Fashion is a fickle thing and is rapidly ever-changing. The speed of change seems to be faster than it has ever been. Not all of us have the spare time in our busy schedules to be reading the latest fashion magazines, or can afford to update an expensive wardrobe every season.

- The fashion industry can make those of us who want to look trendy feel as if we have been left behind. This guide is designed to help women embrace their unique shape and style, make the most of what they have, and share some true style secrets the Fashion industry would rather we didn't know.

- A "Capsule Wardrobe," is a much smaller version of the average overflowing wardrobe, containing smarter and more versatile items. It is a mini wardrobe with a reasonable combination of fashion and style, making it practical for every day use, all occasions and seasons.

- A Capsule Wardrobe can be created by anyone willing to make real positive changes to their image. A successful Capsule Wardrobe not only improves image but also has the potential to improve life in general, improving self confidence and contentment. Embarking on a journey to build a wardrobe that makes sense, not only helps you discover your personal style, it also contributes towards more time and energy to consider and embrace the more important things in life.

- Imagine feeling like you always have something to throw on for all occasions, opening up your wardrobe with the freedom to mix and match. In fact, imagine struggling to choose between outfits simply because they all look good! On top of that, imagine finding yourself with extra cash to treat yourself with or save up, thanks to less money being spent on unnecessary clothing.

Living with less helps reveal the bigger picture in life, potentially bringing about changes beyond what you initially hoped for. Before continuing, I feel there is a significant need to point out that happiness and contentment come from within, not from buying clothes and having a wardrobe to be envied. With that in mind, read on to discover how you can make a step by step plan to make your very own Capsule Wardrobe a reality...

## Chapter 2  Why do you feel like you have nothing to wear?

It is nothing short of ironic when after a big shopping spree, a full wardrobe, and an occasion coming up that is important to you, you find yourself pulling your hair out in search for an outfit that looks and feels just right.   But why?   It's never too late to get to the roots of these common issues women face, and transform your wardrobe into a place you don't dread spending time in.

Before getting stuck into any plans, you will need to be honest with yourself and confront the real reasons there are new clothes in your wardrobe you can't wear, and why you find yourself going back to your old ones. Without a healthy dose of honesty, you might struggle to start taking appropriate action.

Some women find that although buying new clothes seems like a good idea at the time, when they get home and attempt to try on their other existing items with their new ones, it seems next to impossible.

The initial excitement that came with buying a lovely new blouse is shortly followed by a sense of disappointment. Often, this is simply because they did not take into consideration the clothes they already had at home, or what the new item would go with. If you find yourself in a shop for instance, considering a lovely orange blouse, but have a wardrobe so packed you barely know its contents, you might fail to realize in the shop that you actually have nothing that would go well with it.

So you have a wardrobe with brand new clothes in, tags still attached, but by the time you find something that would go well with something else, you either no longer like it, it doesn't fit, or it is too out of fashion to pull off.

Another reason women may feel like they have nothing to wear, despite having a full wardrobe, is because of an unhealthy habit of buying clothes to fulfill emotional needs. Shopping can be an emotional response to certain negative things happening in their lives. If there are any clothes-aholics reading this in hope of breaking free and live in a more minimal fashion, having a consistently good attitude and open mind is a good place to start. Keep reading if you plan on making plans...

"Fail to prepare, prepare to fail."


# Chapter 3   Why Plan?


Planning what steps you will take in order to make your Capsule Wardrobe work is the best way you can start. If you don't make a plan, whether mentally or written, then how can you expect to know what to do and when? In the next section we will be looking at how to create a plan that works well for you. You will be deciding the best way for you to start taking action.

# <u>Chapter 4   Planning:</u>

So you have agreed that making a plan is a good idea, and here you are planning.   First things first, you need to decide a good day to start a wardrobe de-junk. Depending on the size of your wardrobe and the amount of clothes you own, you will need to identify how long you think it will take to de-junk. Deciding how long a de-junk will take varies from one person to the next.

Once you have identified how long it will take, you will then need to decide a good day to begin. A good day to begin should preferably be when you are free from other distracting responsibilities for that amount of time. When you have a time and a date set up, write it on your calendar, put a note on your fridge, or make some sort of note-to-self reminding you of when your wardrobe de-junk will start.

De-junking your wardrobe is the very first and very necessary step to creating your capsule wardrobe. Do not underestimate the importance of this first step, and be prepared for more planning after this step is complete.

# Chapter 5    How to de-junk your wardrobe:

You are reading this now because you are ready to start de-junking your wardrobe.

The first thing you need to do is get your wardrobe completely empty. Make sure that the room you empty your wardrobe in is tidy so you can see where everything is.

Pile all of your clothes/accessories/shoes/bags, you name it, onto your floor or bed.

Once you have everything in a pile, you can start the "weeding" process.

Firstly, you will need to weed out everything that is completely useless or does nothing to benefit your needs.

Your one big pile should eventually turn into smaller piles.

•*A pile for anything that no longer fits, or no longer flatters:*

With each and every item you pick up, it is important to be honest with yourself and have a realistic view. Does it still fit? If it doesn't, then ask yourself why. If something is too big, then its too big. Assuming your not planning to put on weight to wear it, you no longer need it.

Many people who have lost weight struggle with buying clothing in the right size because of an imagine they have in their minds of who they once were. Sometimes, women who are unhappy with their bodies can fall into a trap of buying things for the size they want to be. They convince themselves that they will lose weight if they buy something in a smaller size. The reality of situations like these is that no new outfit has the power to make somebody lose weight, no matter how nice or expensive it is, only the right mindset can lead you in the right direction.

If you weed out things you feel are unflattering, ask yourself why. Some women are not sure what suits them. If your clothes are out of proportion then the overall outfit will be wrong. Things need to be the right length for your body and other items you plan on wearing. When shopping for the right outfits it is important to consider the fit and proportion. Certain colors can also be unflattering to certain skin tones. it is recommended you wear 60% of one color and 40% of another. We will be looking at proportion, fitting, and color, in more detail later on.

•*A pile for anything with price tags still*

*attached that you've owned for too long:*

Some items in your wardrobe may not be saying what you want them to say about you. If you weed out items that have had tags attached for too long, avoid being tempted to keep them in an attempt to "save" the money you spent on them. Consider EBay for selling clothes that are in good wearable condition. If they no longer flatter or fit you, that doesn't mean they won't flatter or fit someone else. Selling your useless clothing could earn you some cash to go towards new clothes that suit you.

•*A pile for fashion items you're waiting to come back in fashion*:

If you bought something on a whim which was fashionable at the time, but is no longer in fashion, waiting for it to come back in is not a wise move. As mentioned earlier, fashion is fickle. There are certain things that never go out of style, which we will be looking at later on. If you are looking at something with a feeling its dated, trust your instincts and put it in the out of fashion pile. Only the timeless classics have stood the test of time. Anything that was once in but is now not, is unlikely to find its way back.

•*A pile for the stained, ripped, faded and tatty:*

A lot of women are surprised to find how much actually lands in this pile. If you have clothes you tell yourself you love too much to let go of, but have undeniable stains or rips on, its time to let go. Alot of the time these clothes go unworn because of these stains or rips, but you tell yourself you will keep them because you like them and will eventually get round to wearing them. You tell yourself you will attempt to repair the rips or remove the stains one day. The truth is if you loved the item that much, you would have attempted to get the stain out or fix the rip as soon a it got there. Be honest with yourself, have you worn the item since the stain or rip? Is the stain there to stay? Are there rips or holes that are not reparable? Is it too obviously faded to wear without it looking old and tatty? There's not a lot you can do about generally faded and tatty clothing or clothing that is beyond repair. Let go and make space for bigger and better things.

•*A pile for things you would wear to do the gardening or housework:*

It doesn't make sense to own more than one outfit you would wear for the messy occasions where its okay to get the rips and stains.

•*A pile for the ridiculous:*

Any clothes that look like you would wear to a costume party...Let go.

•*A pile for the clothes you would be seen dead*

*in:*

Be honest.   If you look at it and think nothing but YUCK, it's time to CHUCK.

If you were honest with yourself, open minded and willing to let go of what needed letting go of, you should be left with the clothes you wear often, or had completely forgotten about but would like to start wearing. You might feel as if you have no clothes left at this point, if this is the case then remind yourself that it is all part of a bigger purpose. You will benefit from taking this step.

The reason I advised piles in certain categories rather than simple throw or keep piles, was to help you discover more about your personal style and unravel what no longer works for you, as well as inspire new looks for the future.

Have a bit of Faith in yourself and trust your instincts, you've got this far so far and will continue to make progress.

**Bonus:**

The clothes saying goodbye to your wardrobe could have you saying hello to some extra cash, or could be donated to a good cause.

# Chapter 6   What certain clothes say about you:

Whether you like it or not, your appearance sends out messages to the outside world.

You may already be aware that your wardrobe can reveal a lot about you.

In this section I would like to encourage you to consider what image you would like to project to others, without putting too much emphasis on what others think. In the end, your aim should be to dress in a way that you feel brings out the best in you.

Studies show that the types of clothes you wear can be subconsciously interpreted by others in certain ways. Thin jumpers for instance, can suggest you are mature and sophisticated, whereas medium-weight knits give a more efficient look.

Some believe that people who wear layers are seen as having more authority.
Research from Australia reveals that a woman wearing a short skirt can come across as open-minded and creative whereas long thin skirts suggest sophistication and intelligence.

Grey is believed to be a color that represents class, efficiency, power and social mobility.

Clothing that tries to hide who you are or shows you didn't pay attention to your situation, body shape, or age, should be avoided.

Studies show that women who are depressed are more likely to wear baggy clothing, whereas women who have a more positive mind frame are more likely to wear a favorite dress, jewelry, or other wardrobe favorites. Studies suggests that women who are feeling low put less effort into what they are wearing, and women who are in a good mood try to dress nicer according to their mood.

Researchers also discovered that a staggering 96% of women believe what they wear effects their confidence levels.

# Chapter 7   How to buy:

Here are some tips to help improve your techniques when it comes to buying clothes when you are shopping. Buying clothes correctly and having the right attitude towards shopping is essential if you are looking to make the right changes to your wardrobe.

- Shopping often and not buying too much is a good way to start. When shopping often you should be looking out for items that would go with everything in your wardrobe. Rather than going over the top and buying everything you think would look great, start by staying on the safe side, slowly but surely building a wardrobe that will eventually balance itself out. If you find items you know go with everything you own and are within your budget, you should consider buying.

- Women often buy what they think they need rather than buying things they love. Sometimes we might think we need a certain item in our wardrobe, but may not necessarily like it.

- This may sound obvious, but it's true. Trying on clothes before buying is a smart move. Sometimes things look more appealing on a hanger than they do on us. And sometimes things look more appealing on us than they do on the hanger. It is always worth trying before buying.

- If you find yourself in a changing area, looking in a mirror with doubts as to whether you actually like what you're wearing, be honest enough with yourself, save some cash and wardrobe space. It may sound obvious, but sometimes simply asking yourself if you love something enough and being true to yourself can make all the difference.

- Visualizing what you have at home and what will go with what you are looking at, can save you time and effort. Unless you are looking to buy an entire outfit from scratch, knowing what you plan to do with your new purchase will have you on the right track.

- If you are planning a shopping trip you know will potentially involve buying clothes, it's a good idea to dress appropriately so that trying on clothes on is as quick and easy as possible.

- A good balanced wardrobe should consist of a combination of high and low brands and designers. One of your goals should be to identify how to spend in the right areas. Beautiful prints, quality shoes and handbags, look as expensive as they are. Know when it's the right time to make an investment, but when it comes to things like leggings and tank tops, stick to the lower price range.

# Chapter 8   Scanning when shopping:

Hopefully you now have a better idea of how to buy more successfully. Shopping for clothes can take a long time as it involves finding styles that suit you, finding the right fit, and working out if items are worth purchasing. In this section we will be looking at how to cut down the time it takes to shop and how to scan for items that suit your needs.

*•Know what you want to buy:*

It will benefit you time-wise to know what you intend to buy before hitting the shops. Whether it be a skirt, suit or shirt. Whatever you plan on buying, keep it in your head and head towards that department. When you are in the right department, stick to that department and focus on what you intend to buy, nothing else.

Then start scanning.

If it's a certain color you are looking for then look only for that color, if you want buttons only then look for buttons only.

Your aim should be to walk into a store and know right away if you are going to find what you are looking for.

*•Know what your price range is:*

Every individual should know what is affordable to them and what their price range is when it comes to shopping for clothes. When you know your set price limit you are then able to know what shops you can afford to buy from. Only go in the shops you know you can afford to scan clothes in, this saves time and energy and narrows down your search.

*•Know your shops:*

If you are looking to buy a sophisticated suit, you should know that TopShop for example, is a pointless place to look. Before you head out, knowing what you have in mind, look into the most suitable stores to start scanning. Do a little research or ask around for some good advice regarding the best places to find what you are looking for. If you have a list of suitable shops either written down or stored in your head, you will feel more organized and will be saving time and possibly frustration. The last thing you want to do is over-complicate a shopping trip by not knowing where you are going and walking around like a headless chicken in search of the unknown.

*•Know the sizes in shops:*

There is nothing more frustrating than finding

just what you're looking for; heading to the changing room with the excitement of seeing how it looks on you, only to discover it does not fit right. This happens to women who are unaware of the different cuts and sizes in different places. Different stores cut to different patterns and European stores generally cut quite small as they are aiming at a young market. TopShop cuts small, whereas Next and M&S cut pretty standard. Gap cuts quite large. When you become familiar with the different cuts in different stores it will be a useful thing to bear in mind when you are on the lookout for your desired purchase.

•*Know what your quality is:*

When you develop enough knowledge, you should be able to scan and spot an ideal buy before you even head to the changing room. Nobody likes getting home to discover their new shoes rub or new clothes creases after ten minutes of wearing.

# Chapter 9   A perfect clothing plan:

When you have a wardrobe that is stored well, you will find that getting dressed and out of the door is a lot less time consuming. Here we will be looking at ways to create a perfectly stored wardrobe.

•*Your Space:*

If you are sharing your wardrobe with your partner, you probably already know that you need more space than him. Women tend to have a lot more clothing than men do. Women tend to have longer clothing than men and typically need two-thirds of space whereas men can make the most of one-third.

•*Folding and Hanging:*

Many of your clothes should be folded rather than hung up. This is a good way to maximize space. Knitted items and T-shirts should be folded as well as other casual items. Anything with creases and sharp edges should be hanging up, and so should anything that needs shape from a hanger to keep its structure, (e.g. Jackets.)

Avoid wire hangers as they are bad for your clothes and can tangle, which makes hanging clothes more awkward that it has to be.

Never hang things in outfits as you will get more wear from your clothes if you hang them separately. It also helps you to be more creative.

Hanging by season will also make your wardrobe a lot easier to organize.

•*Using Storage:*

Use storage techniques that can adapt to the changes of your wardrobe and your storage needs. Using boxes or foldaway storage is a good idea and shoe cubbies can dramatically increase the number of shoes you can keep.   If you have a busy home then having more than one laundry basket will make life easier so you can sort washes by color quicker.

# Chapter 10   Embracing your shape:

Many women struggle with embracing their shape. If you already have, good on you!

Some women struggle due to insecurities which need addressing and some women are simply unaware of how to dress as effectively and according to their shape.

In this section we will be looking at ways you can dress to suit your shape and become confident with what you have.

Each and every one of our bodies is unique. Our body shapes are narrowed down to five general categories but some of you might be a blend between two or more.

These categories are known as:

Apple, Pear, Rectangle, Hourglass and Wedge/Inverted triangle.

## Apple:

*Traits* - Narrow hips with most of your weight

above them. Broad back, ribs and shoulders.

**Best asset** - Legs.

**Goals** - Show off legs and elongate torso.

**Tips...**

- Go for Monochromatic looks.
- Shorter skirts show off legs and and draw attention from mid-section.
- Boot cut jeans and trousers to create even line from shoulders down.
- Wear a bra that gives good lift and support.
- Wear belts at the smallest part of your waist.
- V-neck tops create illusion of longer torso.

## Pear:

**Traits** - Lower body wider than upper body. Hips wider than shoulders. Well-defined waist.

**Best assets** - Shoulders and torso.

**Goals** - Emphasize arms and waist. Add volume to upper body.

**Tips..**

- Pointy toe shoes elongate legs.
- Strapless dresses even out proportions and

show off arms.
- Try A-line shirts and styles with ruffles on top.
- Wear jackets that hit above the waist.
- Keep a look out for boat neck tops, square and cowl necklines.
- Experiment with a light top half and dark bottom half for contrast.
- To balance hips, keep hems of pants, dresses and skirts wide.

# Rectangle:

*Traits -* Waist, hip and shoulders are similar.

*Best assets -* Arms and legs.

*Goals -* Create curves. Show off slender arms and legs.

*Tips...*

- Avoid wearing overwhelming styles.
- Long jackets create lean look.
- Tops with collars, ruffles and other details are flattering to the chest.
- Wear a good bra that makes the most of what you have.
- Scoop necks and sweetheart tops create curves.
- Layers add more dimensions.
- Experiment with colorful bottoms.

# Hourglass:

**_Traits_** - Shoulders and hips in similar proportion. Small waist.

**_Best assets_** - Curves.

**_Goals_** - Show off curves.

**_Tips..._**

- Avoid covering up curves with baggy clothes.
- Wear a good bra to make the most of your bust.
- Wear fitted dresses.
- Wear skinny or straight leg jeans.
- Choose thin, lightweight fabrics and styles.
- Go for high waisted skirts and wear a belt at the waist to enhance shape.

# Wedge/Inverted triangle:

**_Traits_** - Broad chest, wide shoulders, narrow waist and hips.

**_Best Assets_** - Legs.

**_Goals_** - Emphasize lower body and soften upper body.

**_Tips..._**

- Avoid boat neckline tops and spaghetti straps.
- Experiment with high waisted styles.
- Wear full skirts and wide-leg pants.
- Wear bright colors on bottom.
- Search for clothes that create illusion of waist.

# Chapter 11  Timeless trends that never go out of style:

Here is a list of items that will NEVER go out of style.

You would be wise to invest in as many of these as possible and then build on top of the basics each season, keeping your wardrobe minimal yet effective. A good capsule wardrobe should balance between classic and stylish.

## •Prints

Certain prints and patterns will always be smart buys. They are chic, classic and timeless.

You can never go wrong with ***Stripes.*** They are incredibly versatile. A good striped skirt or dress definitely deserves a place in your wardrobe.

***Polka Dots,*** another print that will be forever fashionable. Dotted clothes and accessories such as scarves and cardigans are the safest to pull off. You might find bags and purses less versatile but overall the possibilities with polka dots can be endless.

If you are looking to go for a feminine, pretty look, then ***Florals*** are definitely your friends.

As with dots, floral prints can vary according to what the experts declare is on trend, but there are so many items that can look lovely in floral. Florals were long considered to be for the spring and summer, but winter florals have been on trend for many years now and will be for many to come. Finding floral prints you love and that suit you timelessly are keepers.

**Leopard Print** can be controversial when it comes to the message it sends off, some believing it gives the impression of fast, easy women lacking morals. Most younger folks, however, are open to animal prints in its many forms, including leopard print. Leopard is a print that can be worn all year round and is also loved in many forms and accessories.

**Tartan** is a cute chic classic. It may seem too autumnal for all year round, but it most certainly makes it on most retail racks by winter. If chosen right, there is no reason it cannot be worn through winter and spring. A nice light weight button up tartan shirt can be pulled off come rain or shine. Its hard to find accessories that look timelessly trendy in tartan, but overall you will never find a year its not considered chic.

If you are looking for a slightly bolder statement and want to stand out from the crowd, then **Houndstooth** is a great option. There is undeniable power in black and white prints but Houndstooth is on the next level. It also adds a dash of masculine influence to any outfit and looks great with natural looking florals. Again, a timeless print which is worth investing in if it suits your style.

## •Little black dress

What woman isn't thankful for this iconic, genius creation? Its Coco Chanel we should be grateful to for this dress that has it all. Before the 1920's black was worn by women mostly to represent a time of mourning. Now the little black dress is the one dress we can never go wrong with, it is possible to wear all year round, every season, and look well dressed. So many looks can be created with the little black dress. Holly Golightly in Breakfast at Tiffanys, played by Audrey Hepburn, started a real trend. It really took off after the movie and has been iconic ever since.

Go for a simple, elegant little black dress, something that is timeless and free from the limits of current fashion trends. Your little black dress should stand the test of time. When it comes to a wardrobe staple such as this it is important to think of fit, proportions and style. Think quality and not quantity.

*"One is never overdressed or underdressed with a little black dress."*
*—Karl Lagerfeld*

## •Jeans

There are so many different types of jeans out there that we are spoiled for choice. They are a must have capsule wardrobe essential for every woman. A good pair of jeans can transform any look. Skinny jeans are not just for the "skinny," they can look good on all shapes and sizes if worn right and they work every season. From high wasted flairs to holes on the knees, Denim will never go out of fashion and there will always be something for everyone.

## •Pencil skirt

Pencil skirts are timeless classics. Skirts symbolize a women's grace and elegance and most icons wore a pencil skirt at some point or another. Choose the right color to suit your every day looks, black is sexy and sophisticated but its good to be individual. A pencil skirt goes with anything, from chiffon blouses and lace tops to plain loose fitted tees. There are so many patterns, prints, colors and styles to choose from so have fun with it.

## •Simple white Tee

Everyone should know that a simple plain white tee is a must have wardrobe essential. There are so many things you can do with this one item with a little imagination. A plain white tee teamed up with some smart accessories can bring an outfit to life. Plain white tees go with everything from skirts and jeans to shorts, not to mention all materials from denim and leather to suede. Whatever you have in your wardrobe you will never struggle to find an outfit if your trusted plain white tee is in there. Just make sure it's a good quality one so you can happily wear it time and time again, without ever worrying about it going out of style!

## •Collar shirts

Collar shirts will always be something you can find in retail stores. They date all the way back to an old fashioned time but are still considered trendy. They are designed in many different ways with or without buttons and can worn by both men and women. They are good for brooches, necklaces and ties.

## •Trench coat

A trench coat is a classic that will never go out of style. Whether you're on a budget or are looking to make an investment, a trench coat is another must have for every woman's capsule wardrobe. They are so effortlessly chic and versatile and come in endless styles, colors and lengths. There is a trench coat out there for every woman regardless of frame or height. Trench coats can create so many different looks and can be worn with a range of different outfits.

## •Button down shirts

These shirts are universally flattering. There are so many cuts and styles to choose from and they are appropriate for all occasions from work to a date. These shirts can be styled with most items from the classic pencil skirt to jeans. There are so many options with this shirt, it can be fully buttoned up or left open for potential layering. A button down shirt will never go out of style and definitely deserves a place in your wardrobe.

## •Blazer

The ever-classic blazer will never be out of style, and again there is so much variety out there that you should have fun finding your perfect blazer. A blazer can also be worn for different occasions from work to play; they can be smart or casual. There are many looks a blazer can portray.

# Chapter 12   Wardrobe staples and signature items:

Here we will be looking at what wardrobe staples and signature items actually are, before working out how to find your very own.

We have already looked at trends that never go out of style, and by now you should have made some interesting discoveries when it comes to the clothes that are going in your new wardrobe. I hope you have discovered more about your personal style and feel more confident when it comes to being true to that style.

Style is personal and timeless. It is important for your style to develop, to change, and to evolve as time goes by. It should also remain consistent with your personal identity.

If you have a special piece of clothing, or an accessory that is personal to you and your style, then that could be considered a signature item. A wardrobe staple is an item you would never consider parting with, it belongs is your wardrobe and it is there to stay, even if that means replacing it at some point down the line.

If you have fallen in love with certain items, (whatever they may be) and you feel they are an essential expression of your personal style, then those items are your signature items.

A signature item can be anything from a perfume to a watch. It is anything that you know represents your style so well that you can't imagine being without it.

Some items have character and can say a lot about you.

If you already own a signature item or wardrobe staple then you will understand where I am coming from, whether you do or don't own one or more already, take a look at what to bear in mind when in search for a signature piece:

# •Timelessness

By now you know what it means to own a timeless piece. A signature item should definitely be timeless so as the years goes by you will remain forever glad to own.

# •Versatility

A good classic goes with anything and everything else.

### •Character

The best items come with a story to tell.

### •Quality

Quality is a key element. Look for a piece that ages beautifully and endures time well.

### •Value for money

Even if the piece you have your heart set on will cause a momentary financial setback, the cost of a classic will serve you long enough for you to look back and be thankful for the investment.

# Chapter 13   Successful accessorizing:

It is said that 25% of a women's wardrobe budget should go towards accessories.

Accessorizing successfully can save you money and time, not to mention it can boost your confidence levels.

If you own enough of the right accessories, then you won't have to buy as many clothes.

For the most part, your wardrobe is driven by the basics. It is successfully accessorizing that has the power to change your looks. Accessories are often cheaper than clothes and can be worn multiple times during the week. If you owned one dress but lots of accessories you could wear that dress in different ways simply by changing your jewelry or shoes.

Time is saved with accessorizing. It can give one piece multiple looks and takes a lot less time during your busy mornings than struggling to work out what outfit to put together.

Not only does getting smart with your accessories save you time and money, it can also help you stand out from the crowd a bit more, in a good way.

A lack of accessories can make you feel dull and boring. If two women are wearing a button down shirt and pair of tailored pants, the one who is going to stand out the most will be the one who chooses to finish her look with a great necklace and interesting pair of shoes. Maybe some colorful jewelry and a handbag that isn't dull.

The possibilities with accessorizing are endless. If you learn to do it right you could end up feeling a lot better about yourself too.

Feeling good about yourself comes from within, and if you know you are successfully expressing who you are on the inside through your accessories, people may well get to know who you are more easily just by your presence.

Start working on how you present yourself on the outside and you inner confidence will shine.

### *Here are some top tips for successful accessorizing:*

•Keep a jewelry box containing accessories that will never go out of style.

•Own a mixture of both silver and gold basic chains.

- When it comes to heavier metal stick to metals that best suit your skin tone. (Fair and rosy skin often suit silver the most whereas complexions with a yellow tint usually look best in gold.)

- Own at least one basic pendant necklace.

- Invest in earring posts for hoops, dangling earrings and studs (if you have pierced ears.)

- A good watch is a wise investment and a timeless item. Go for one with a metal or leather band. Avoid plastic straps.

- Keep one nice tennis bracelet.

- Search for classic stones such as diamonds and pearls.

- Experiment with colored jewelry but don't go over the top. If you're wearing all black, a bold colored scarf, jacket or bag could spice things up and create a great looking outfit.

- Investment in a great bag + a great pair of shoes = success.

- Belts are very versatile accessories. Narrow belts can glam up dresses or accent the narrow part of your waist whereas wide elastic belts can turn something from slouchy to chic in seconds and flatter your figure

# Chapter 14   Colors:

What do colors convey?

The colors you choose to wear can say a lot about your personality, especially in the world of work. Here we are going to take a look at what different colors represent and how to choose the right colors to bring out the best in you.

Dark colors convey authority and power. Black and navy blue are the most popular dark colors to wear. Pastel colors are relaxed and friendly and mixed colors convey creativity.

## Red

Reds can vary when it comes to the message they send off. A strong red is the color to choose if you are looking to draw attention to yourself, it is said that women who wear red come across as confident. Red is the color of of energy and symbol of life, it grabs our attention and creates a visual impact. Burgundy on the other hand is considered a color of sophistication. Beware of red coming across as aggressive; it is a very bold color.

## Yellow

Yellow is a warm and optimistic color. It is associated with happiness, light and laughter. Yellow can bring out a cheerful feeling in us and is also said to have the power to bring out creativity. The right shade of yellow can represent a friendly nature but can be overpowering if too much is used or if it is too bright.

## Green

Green is a color that represents nature and money, it is also a calming color associated with generosity and peace. It is also considered to be the color of restoration and balance as it is located in the center of the color spectrum.

## Blue

Some shades of blue can evoke coldness but overall it is a peaceful, calming and restful color. Research suggests that people can be more productive when working in a blue room as it helps them to stay focused and calm. Blue is many people's favorite color, it is associated with trust, serenity, intelligence and sufficiency.

## Orange

Orange is a bold color that can make you feel quite playful. It has also been said that orange has a sexual energy to it. It is a color associated with warmth, fun and ambition. There is nothing soothing about this color. If you are looking to make a bold statement but you're sick of red, then orange is the one for you.

## Purple

Purple is the color of royalty. It is associated with wealth, wisdom and sophistication. Purple is a classy color that can also convey prosperity and spiritual awareness. If you are looking to convey quality then this is a good color but too much overpowering purple can come across as immature.

## Pink

Pink conveys an open heart. It is considered loving, warm and tranquil. It is known to be one of the most feminine colors. Did you know the cells of some of the most dangerous criminals are painted pink? This is because it has been shown to calm aggression. Pink is soothing unlike red which is stimulating.

Black is a color that represents authority,

sophistication, strength and power. It is a somber color that it is associated with intelligence. It can be overwhelming if worn from head to toe as it is a serious color. It is said that black is every color in one, it conceals and enshrouds.

White is the opposite of black. It symbolizes new beginnings and a fresh outlook. Whites, browns and beige's that come close to your natural skin tone can really compliment you.

Whatever colors you choose to wear, it is recommended that you do not wear too much of one color at once. It can be overwhelming and give off the wrong impression. Not everyone has their favorite colors in common with each other. Showing a good balance with your color choices gives off a better impression than being totally absorbed in a single color or a color standing out more than you do. As mentioned earlier, 60% of one color and 40% of another is a good balance.

It can be fun choosing different shades too. Shades make a significant difference to color. A dark, forest green, for example, has a totally different effect than a pastel or lime green. Bright pink, for example, has a totally different effect than a soft light pink.

Choose colors that you feel represent your style best but balance those colors out with neutral colors such as black, white and browns.

# Chapter 15   Occasions:

There are many occasions we find ourselves needing to dress for in life.

Whether it be a wedding, every day work wear or a casual day out, dressing in style for all occasions is something you can do successfully.

By now you should know what essentials your wardrobe should contain and know how to make certain looks work for you.

In this section we are going to look at how to dress casually, how to dress for work and how to dress when dressing up to go out.

## *Work*

Every work setting or office is different. Here is a guide that is applicable to almost any workplace setting.

•If you want to wear something bold on the lower half of your body, such as a bold printed pair of trousers or skirt, balance it with something more polished looking like a crisp white blouse.

•Avoid going shorter than three inches above the knee when it comes to skirts. The safest hemline is at the knee.

•If you are going for a very sheer top, be on the safe side and wear a camisole underneath. Also top it with a blazer.

•Don't go overboard with mixing prints. Floral and subtle stripes work well.

•Make sure that all items are as wrinkle-free as you can get them. Your whole outfit should be well pressed.

•If ever in doubt, do wear your pumps.

•Avoid spaghetti straps, sleeveless tops should extend to the edges of your shoulders.

•Do not allow your neckline to go any lower than four inches below your collarbone.

# *Play*

Away from work we all have a life, and from time to time we have places to go which require a bit of dressing up. The first thing you should bear in mind is that it's OK to have a bit of fun with it. Feel free to experiment every now and then, being comfortable is key.

• Take into consideration where it is you are going and give yourself some time to think about outfit ideas.

• Check out books, magazines or browse online for inspiration.

• For extra special occasions, consider getting your hair done professionally at a salon.

• Choose makeup that compliments your outfit and skin tone, avoid wearing too much.

• Don't be afraid of a bold colored lipstick if the

rest of your look is significantly neutral or dark.

•To accessorize for a special occasion, choose your best jewelry but make sure it matches.

•Choose something that modestly shows off your assets.

•Go for something that brings out your inner style and inner confidence.

•If wearing heels, choose a pair you are comfortable in that won't lead to blisters. You'll thank yourself later on.

•If in doubt, stick with the little black dress and accessorize with it.

## *Casual*

Unless you're a bit of a party animal, out of work hours usually consist of a more casual look.

Most of the clothes which work for every day casual wear should be a part of your new capsule wardrobe. Let's take a closer look at how these casual essentials can work for any day of the week.

### •Sweater

A sweater that's right up your street is a good item to invest in for the days you don't intend to look dressy. They can be worn on their own or layered on top of other clothes. They come in different shapes, sizes and styles.

### •Jeans/Slacks

A pair of plain denim jeans or slacks should go well with any top half you wish to create. If you're looking to go for a slightly bolder lower half then keep the upper half more neutral.

### •Overalls

These look great with a classic plain tee and a pair of casual pumps or sneakers. A cute and versatile look which you can have fun with. They come in different colors and materials, long legged and short. A pair of cool denim overalls go well with most colors, so despite the plain white tee looking great with them, your options do not end there.

### •Flat shoes

Flats can be glamorous and go with virtually anything. They are a great way to give your legs a break, and your feet if you're used to wearing heels on a regular basis.

•Neutrals

Neutral shades give off a casual vibe and can make you feel more relaxed and laid back. We do need time off sometimes from being so stylish!

# Chapter 16   Learn from your mistakes:

I hope you enjoyed this journey with me and have learned a valuable thing or two along the way.   I would like to finish off by pointing out that everyone make mistakes from time to time when it comes to their dress sense, no matter how much of an expert they may consider themselves to be. The point is we learn from our mistakes and grow from them.

As your sense of style matures, your mistakes will occur less often. Never give up on dressing to bring out the best in yourself or think any less of yourself when mistakes are made.

We all look back at some point or another and think "What was I thinking?"

Dressing well has a lot to do with your taste level and beginners need to learn some lessons before their style can fully mature.

Avoid falling into the trap of telling yourself your style sucks over a little error, simply because you need more practice with discovering what works for you and learning what doesn't.

Every single one of us has something individual to offer and in the end it's not about how we look on the outside that counts, it's how we feel on the inside.

The more content you are with who you are, the easier you will find moving on from your mistakes quickly, transforming from a capsule wardrobe caterpillar to a beautifully stylish butterfly!

CPSIA information can be obtained
at www.ICGtesting.com
Printed in the USA
LVOW07s1139141017
552442LV00016B/315/P

9 781533 491534